Tell Me About Dinosaurs
VELOCIRAPTOR

Marjorie Seevers

xist Publishing

Velociraptor was a small dinosaur.

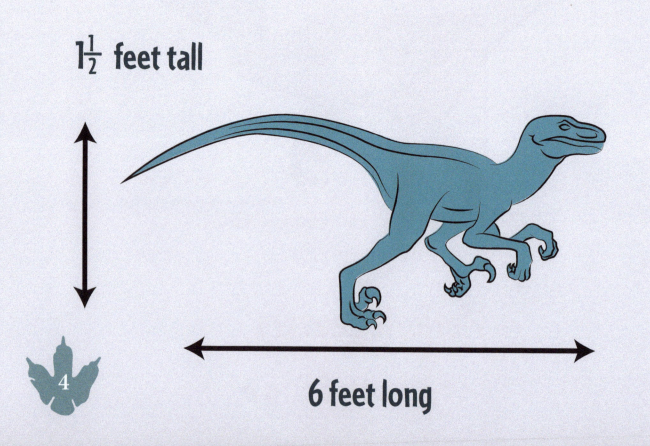

$1\frac{1}{2}$ feet tall

6 feet long

Check out all of the books in the Tell Me About Dinosaurs Series

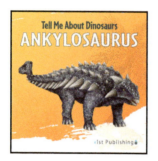
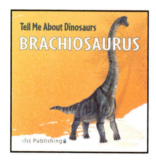
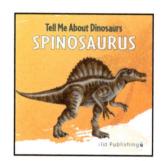
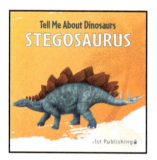
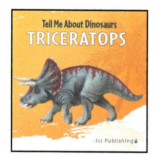
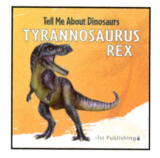
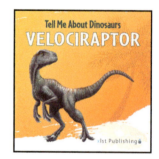

Published in the United States by Xist Publishing
www.xistpublishing.com
© 2025 Copyright Xist Publishing

All rights reserved
No portion of this book may be reproduced without express permission of the publisher.
All images licensed from Adobe Stock

First Edition
Hardcover ISBN: 978-1-5324-5511-7
Paperback ISBN: 978-1-5324-5512-4
eISBN: 978-1-5324-5510-0

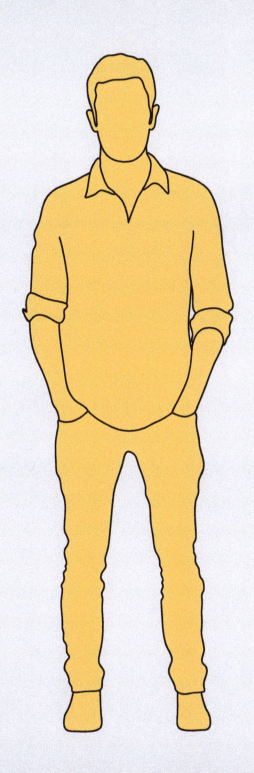

It ate meat.

Velociraptor had sharp claws.

VELOCIRAPTOR

CRETACEOUS
MONGOLIA

'TRIASSICA'

It had a long, curved claw on each foot.

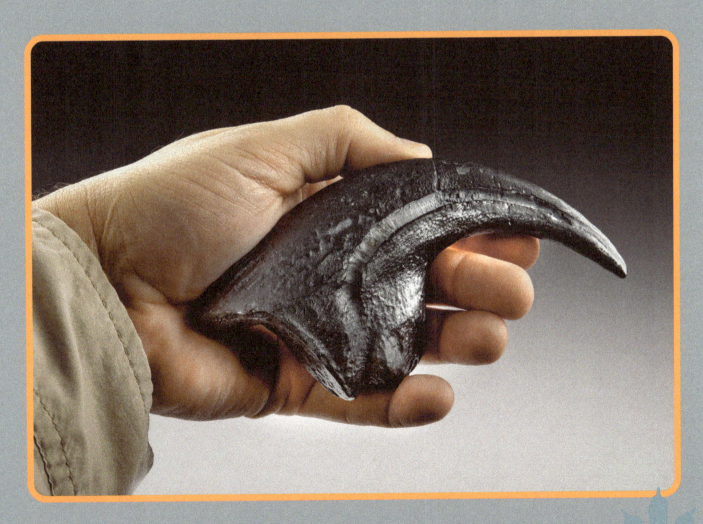

Velociraptor was very fast.

Some scientists think it had feathers.

Velociraptor bones are called fossils.

Which dinosaur is a Velociraptor?

What did Velociraptor eat?

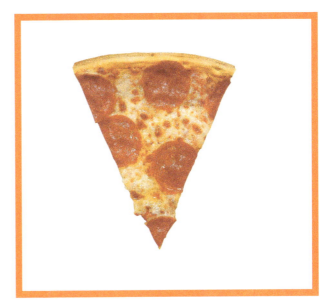

www.ingramcontent.com/pod-product-compliance
Ingram Content Group UK Ltd.
Pitfield, Milton Keynes, MK11 3LW, UK
UKHW050136080425
457124UK00014B/105